5&1 DIET PLANS AND RECIPES

THE EASIEST AND HEALTHIEST WAY TO GET YOUR

SHAPE BACK

WITHOUT STRESS

Annalisa Williams

© Copyright 2021 by Annalisa Williams – All rights reserved.

The following Book is reproduced below with the goal of providing information that is as accurate and reliable as possible.

Regardless, purchasing this Book can be seen as consent to the fact that both the publisher and the author of this book are in no way experts on the topics discussed within and that any recommendations or suggestions that are made herein are for entertainment purposes only.

Professionals should be consulted as needed prior to undertaking any of the action endorsed herein.

This declaration is deemed fair and valid by both the American Bar Association and the Committee of Publishers Association and is legally binding throughout the United States.

Furthermore, the transmission, duplication, or reproduction of any of the following work including specific information will be considered an illegal act irrespective of if it is done electronically or in print.

This extends to creating a secondary or tertiary copy of the work or a recorded copy and is only allowed with the express written consent from the Publisher. All additional right reserved.

The information in the following pages is broadly considered a truthful and accurate account of facts and as such, any inattention, use, or misuse of the information in question by the reader will render any resulting actions solely under their purview.

There are no scenarios in which the publisher or the original author of this work can be in any fashion deemed liable for any hardship or damages that may befall them after undertaking information described herein.

Additionally, the information in the following pages is intended only for informational purposes and should thus be thought of as universal.

As befitting its nature, it is presented without assurance regarding its prolonged validity or interim quality.

Trademarks that are mentioned are done without written consent and can in no way be considered an endorsement from the trademark holder.

TABLE OF CONTENT

INTRODUCTION 10
WHAT 5&1 DIET CONSIST? 16
WHY IS 5&1 DIET SO EFFECTIVE IN LOSING WEIGHT? 19
WHY 5&1 DIET RATHER THAN OTHER DIET? .. 25
LEAN AND GREEN RECIPES 29
- DELICIOUS ZUCCHINI QUICHE 31
- CLOUD BREAD 33
- AVOCADO LIME SHRIMP SALAD 35

FUELING RECIPES 37
- HIGH PROTEIN CHIPOTLE CHEDDAR QUESADILLA 39
- ZUCCHINI BOATS WITH BEEF AND PIMIENTO ROJO 41
- CARROT CAKE OATMEAL 43
- SPICED SORGHUM AND BERRIES 44
- BEST WHOLE WHEAT PANCAKES 45

BREAKFAST 47
- WALNUT CRUNCH BANANA BREAD 49
- PLANT- POWERED PANCAKES 50
- LEAN AND GREEN CHICKEN PESTO PASTA 51
- CRUNCHY QUINOA MEAL 53
- COCONUT PANCAKES 54
- ZUCCHINI PANCAKES 55
- SQUASH HASH 57

MAINS 59

HERBED WILD RICE 61
BUFFALO CHICKEN SLIDERS 62
HERBED GARLIC BLACK BEANS 63
QUINOA WITH VEGETABLES 64
GREEK STYLE QUESADILLAS 65
LIGHT PAPRIKA MOUSSAKA 66
PROSCIUTTO WRAPPED MOZZARELLA BALLS 68

SNACKS RECIPES 69

EGGPLANT DIP 71
BULGUR LAMB MEATBALLS 72
CUCUMBER ROLLS 73
FETA ARTICHOKE DIP 74
CHEESEBURGER PIE 75
CHICKEN AND MUSHROOMS 77
BAKED BEEF ZUCCHINI 78
COBB SALAD WITH BLUE CHEESE DRESSING 80

VEGETABLES 83

SWEET POTATO CHIPS 85
FRIED ZUCCHINI 86
CAULIFLOWER CRUST PIZZA 88
THAI ROASTED VEGGIES 90
CRISPY-TOPPED BAKED VEGETABLES 91

MEAT 93

TOMATO BRAISED CAULIFLOWER WITH CHICKEN 95
CUMIN-LIME STEAK 97
MEDITERRANEAN GRILLED CHICKEN 98

SOUPS 101

QUICK LENTIL CHILI 103

LEMON GARLIC OREGANO CHICKEN WITH ASPARAGUS 104
EASY CAULIFLOWER SOUP 105

SMOOTHIES 107

CANTALOUPE KALE SMOOTHIE 109
MIX BERRY CANTALOUPE SMOOTHIE 110
SOURSOP SMOOTHIE 111
CUCUMBER-GINGER WATER 112

DESSERTS 113

GRANOLA 115
DELICIOUS BROWNIE BITES 116
PUMPKIN BALLS 117
CHOCOLATE FROSTY 118
PEANUT BUTTER FUDGE 119
EASTER BUNNY 120

INTRODUCTION

The importance of a healthy diet for our health is always well known. Hippocrates said "Your food is your remedy" and "The way you eat determines the state of your health".

The great dilemma remains the choice of the right diet to follow for a good state of health.

Scientific studies in the field of nutrition confirm that fattening is not only due to the number of calories consumed but also to the inflammation that food can cause.

A sad truth is the fact that overweight and obesity are chronic inflammatory diseases, it has been abundantly demonstrated by scientific studies that inflammation in general, and in particular BAFF (one of the inflammatory cytokines most related to food) determine insulin resistance. A food reaction that generates inflammation (as in the case of food intolerances) triggers in the body an inflammatory process that causes weight gain and especially fat mass.

In order to have a good weight loss and improve our lifestyle it is important to follow a diet that includes healthy eating habits but also the immunological reality of the subject, evaluating food hypersensitivity, in a nutshell we must find out which food is responsible for inflammation.
Keep in mind that a diet that controls inflammation from food (food intolerances) favors weight loss, decreasing above all the fat mass without affecting the

lean mass, which would cause a decrease in metabolism.

There are different types of fats, the ones that we should prefer are the "healthy" fats or polyunsaturated fatty acids contained in oils and fish, especially in the blue one rich in linolenic and linoleic acid (better known as omega-3 and omega-6).

Do not underestimate the amount of vitamin E contained in good oils that counteracts the 'negative effect carried out by free radicals.

For the reasons listed above we believe that whole foods and vegetable oils are essential for our health, and it would be ideal to include them in all meals. Same thing with carbohydrates, it is recommended to consume more whole carbohydrates. For example, pasta, prepared with semolina, maintains a low glycemic index, so it can be included among the foods to be favored and not among those to be limited.

Speaking of proteins, the recommended method is to consume every day about 1 gram of protein per kilogram of body weight (the recommended weight in relation to height, sex and age). The foods richest in protein are definitely meat (approximately 22-25 grams per 100 grams of meat), fish (approximately 17-20 grams per 100 grams), legumes (dried lentils contain about 22-23 grams of protein per 100 grams of weight).

On alcohol the thought of doctors is divided, it is assumed that, in the absence of contraindications, moderate consumption of alcohol does not harm our organism, and would help reduce cardiovascular risk. Then talking about vitamin supplements experts say that by eating fruits and vegetables regularly our body assimilates plenty of vitamins and minerals.

The 5&1 Diet has been subjected to various studies to Prove its efficacy in weight loss. Different studies were published in various journals indicating that those who follow this Program are able to see significant changes in as little as 8 weeks and that People can achieve their long-term health goals with the 5&1Diet.

While the initial 5&1 ideal weight Plan is quite restrictive, maintenance Phases 3&3 allow for greater variety of less Processed foods and snacks, which can facilitate weight loss.
Under this diet regimen, dieters are required to follow a weight Plan that includes five fueling a day and one lean green meal daily. However, there are also other regimens of this Diet if the five fuels a day is too much for you.
The diet is a set of three Programs, two of which focus on weight loss and one that is best for weight maintenance, if you are not trying to lose weight. The Plans are high in Protein and low in carbohydrates and calories to stimulate weight loss.

If you are interested in trying this, consider working with an experienced registered dietitian who can help you stay Properly fed   as you strive to achieve your desired weight.
For the most desirable 5 and 1 weight Plan, eat 5 foods Per day, Plus a low carb lean meal and a low carb elective snack.
Although Initial Plan 5 & 1 is reasonably restrictive, Protection Segment 3 & 3 allows for a greater variety of less Processed foods and snacks, which can also make weight loss easier and more Persistent for long Period.
The bottom line is, that the 5&1 weight loss Plan Promotes weight loss via low calorie Prepackage meals; low carb homemade food, and Personalized

coaching; at the same time, as this system Promotes quick-time Period weight and fat loss, similarly research is wanted to assess whether it encourages the everlasting way of life adjustments needed for long-time Period achievement.

WHAT 5&1 DIET CONSIST?

The 5&1 Diet has been subjected to various studies to prove its efficacy in weight loss. Different studies were published in various journals indicating that the subjects who follow this Program are able to get amazing changes in 8 weeks and achieve their long-term health goals with selected diet plans.

While the initial 5&1 ideal weight Plan is quite restrictive, maintenance Phases 3&3 allow for greater variety of less Processed foods and snacks, which can facilitate weight loss.
Under this diet regimen, dieters are required to follow a weight Plan that includes five fueling a day and one lean green meal daily. However, there are also other regimens of this Diet if the five fuels a day is too much for you.
The diet is a set of three Programs, two of which focus on weight loss and one that is best for weight maintenance, if you are not trying to lose weight. The Plans are high in Protein and low in carbohydrates and calories to stimulate weight loss.

If you are interested in trying this, consider working with an experienced registered dietitian who can help you stay Properly fed as you strive to achieve your desired weight.
For the most desirable 5 and 1 weight Plan, eat 5 foods Per day, Plus a low carb lean meal and a low carb elective snack.
Although Initial Plan 5 & 1 is reasonably restrictive, Protection Segment 3 & 3 allows for a greater variety of less Processed foods and snacks, which can also

make weight loss easier and more Persistent for long Period.
The bottom line is, that the 5&1 weight loss Plan Promotes weight loss via low calorie Prepackage meals; low carb homemade food, and Personalized coaching; at the same time, as this system Promotes quick-time Period weight and fat loss, similarly

How It Works

The 5&1 diet focus to reduce or maintain current weight. It is a diet that recommends eating a combination of processed foods called fuels and home-cooked meals (lean and green meals). It is believed that it sticks to the brand Product (input) and supplements it with meat, vegetables, and fatty snacks; this process will maintain you satisfied all day. At the same you do not need to worry much about losing muscles because you are having enough Protein and consuming too few calories.
And that way, the individual who Practices the diet can lose around 12 Pounds in just 12 weeks using the ideal 5&1 weight Plan.
So basically the 5&1 diet is a Program that focuses on cutting calories and reducing carbohydrates in meals. To do this effectively, combine Packaged foods called fuels with home-cooked meals, which encourages weight loss.
Users Pick the Plan that best suits them.
The 5 & 1 Plan entails eating five small meals Per day. The meals can be selected from more than 60 substitutable fuels, including one "lean and green" meal, Probably veggies or protein that you will prepare by yourself.

WHY IS 5&1 DIET SO EFFECTIVE IN LOSING WEIGHT?

Most "supplies" contain between 100 and 110 calories each, which means you can consume around 1000 calories a day on this diet. As a result of this approach, the US News and World Report ranked it second on its list of the best diets for fast weight loss, but 32nd on its list of the best diets for healthy eating. London recognizes that there are other ways to lasting weight loss: "Eat meals and snacks that incorporate lots of Products, seeds, nuts, greens, 100% whole grains, eggs, seafood, Poultry, greens, low-fat dairy Products. Fat, lean meat Plus a little indulgence is the best way to lose weight sustainably in the long run.

"So will the 5&1 diet help you lose weight?
The amount of weight you lose after following this diet Programs depends on factors such as your starting weight, as well as your activity and loyalty to following the Plan.
Little specific research has been Published on the 5&1 brand. The studies, like most diets, were small, with numerous dropouts. Research seems to confirm this. On the other hand, the long-term expectation is less Promising.
Here's a more detailed look at the data:
According to a 2017 5&1's sponsored study, more than 70% of overweight adults who received individual behavioral support and underwent 5&1 have lost more than 5% of their body weight since their last visit, which is four to 24 weeks. then.

According to a 2016 study Published in the journal Obesity and with Partial support from the 5&1

Research Team, obese adults lost 8.8% of their body weight after 12 weeks with 5&1 style training, and also 12,1% of your body weight if you were taking Phentermine at the same time, which is a weight loss drug that can reduce binge eating.

However, the researchers found only one long-term study, which indicated no benefit for these 12-month Plans. The researchers found that there is also an increased risk of complications, such as gallstones, on ultra-low-calorie Programs.

However, the study found that the effect was reduced beyond six months of reporting the results.

During a small study, designed and funded by Sallige Institution and Published in 2010 in the Nutrition Journal, 90 obese adults were randomly assigned to either the low-calorie diet or the 5 & 1 Plan according to government guidelines. The 5&1 dieters, however, regained more than 4.5 kg 24 weeks later, after the calories gradually increased. The others gained only 2 Pounds. Comparted to the initial exercise, the 5&1 group had more muscle mass and less body fat at week 40, but it did not outperform the control group. Eventually, about half of the 5&1 group and more than half of the control group withdrew.

According to a Sallige-funded study of 119 overweight or obese type 2 diabetics Published in Diabetes Educator in 2008, dieters were randomly assigned to either a 5&1 diabetes Plan or a diet based on the recommendations of the American Association of Diabetes.

After 34 weeks, the 5&1 group had lost an average of 4.5 kilos, but had regained almost 1.5 kilos after 86 weeks. Over 34 weeks, those who followed the ADA-based diet lost an average of 3 Pounds; they got everything back Plus an extra Pound in 86 weeks. By the end of the year, about 80% had given up

According to an analysis Published in 2008 in the journal Eating and Weight Disorders, researchers analyzed the medical records of 324 People who were on a diet who were overweight or obese and who were also taking a Prescription appetite suppressant. In 12 weeks, they lost an average of 21 Pounds, in 24 weeks they weighed 26 1/2 Pounds, and 27 Pounds in 52 weeks.

Furthermore, for approximately 80% of them, at least 5% of the initial weight had been lost in all three evaluations. This is great if you are obese, because losing just 5-10% of your current weight can help prevent some diseases.

However, these numbers are accompanied by some asterisks. First, because they are based on people who completed the 52-week Program, they were more likely to lose weight. (Weight loss was still effective, but less Pronounced in a cessation analysis.)

Second, a review of Patient data is given less importance than a study with a control group. Finally, in a survey in which researchers divided dieters into consumer groups on Sallige, those who recognized that they consume at least two shakes a day at each check-in and those who are inconsistent, it is say, the rest. , weight loss was not significantly different.

In a 2013 study in the International Journal of Obesity that looked at 120 men and women ages 19 to 65, half of whom were using 5&1, while the other half were limited to cutting calories, researchers found that those who on the 5&1 diet lost an average of 16 1/2 Pounds after 26 weeks, compared to the control group, who lost 4 kg.

The 5&1 diet has generated headlines throughout the year. Users must enroll in a low-calorie meal

Plan and then Purchase the Packaged foods that are Part of the chosen plan.

No food group is completely off limits, Promising "Permanent transformation, one healthy habit at a time."

Although it has many fans, this diet is not cheap. The US News and World Report ranked it second in the rapid weight loss category. In 2018, it was also a Popular diet on Google. Famous "cake chef" Buddy Valastro credits 5&1 for his recent weight loss.

Do you want to try the 5&1 diet? Will this really help you lose weight? Here's everything for you: the health implications, if they are difficult to follow, and the likelihood of reaching your weight loss goal.

WHY 5&1 DIET RATHER THAN OTHER DIET?

Calorie Restriction Impact
Despite the fact that 5&1's eating routine arrangement stresses eating every now and again for the duration of the day, every one of its "fuels" just gives 110 calories. "Lean and green" foods are additionally low in calories.
At the Point when you're eating fewer calories all in all, you may discover the arrangement leaves you ravenous and unsatisfied. You may likewise feel all the more effectively exhausted and even crabby.
Weariness and Isolation at Mealtimes
5&1's dependence on meal substitutions can meddle with the social Parts of getting ready and eating food. Clients may think that it's clumsy or baffling to have a shake or bar at family supper time or when feasting out with companions.
How It Compares with others The 5&1 Diet can be more viable for fast weight reduction than different Plans basically in view of what a limited number of calories its fuels and "lean and green" meals give.
U.S. News and World report Positioned 5&1 as the number two best eating routine for quick weight reduction (attached with Atkins, keto, and Weight Watchers).1

The 2019 U.S. News and World report Best Diets Positioned the 5&1 Diet 31st in Best Diets Overall and gave it a general score of 2.7/5.
This diet requires less "mental acrobatic" than contenders like Weight Watchers, (for which you need

to gain Proficiency with an arrangement of focuses) or keto (for which you should intently follow and evaluate macronutrients).

5&1's instructing segment is similar to Weight Watchers and Jenny Craig, the two of which urge members to select in for meetups to get social help. The exceptionally handled nature of most nourishments you'll eat on the 5&1 diet can be a drawback contrasted with the variety of new, entire nourishments you can eat on increasingly Independently directed Plans, for example, Atkins. Calorie restriction is essential to weight reduction and the 5&1 option is Particularly conducive to shedding weight rapidly with an 800-one thousand calorie nutritional Plan. Carbs also are stored low with a decent amount of Protein Per serving which is right for effective weight reduction in maximum instances. Plus, carb and calorie restrict have shown to have many health advantages which includes advanced glucose metabolism, adjustments in frame composition, reduced danger of cardiovascular chance elements, and other disorder chance elements as nicely.

But the 5&1 may not be for anyone as dropping weight quickly and excessive calorie restrict can be damaging to your health and also you virtually won't experience excellent, at the same time as muscle loss is likewise an opportunity. 800-one thousand energy are quite low, in standard.

However, for weight loss, eating 800-1000 energy can be safe and effective if no longer applied for extended Periods.

Research suggests that too few calories can have an effect on metabolism over the years that could make you to regain weight.

But this will additionally be due to long term habits as there are also several different variables to recall in

terms of the differences among people. Weight loss isn't continually easy and retaining it off may be even more difficult however it requires everlasting lifestyle changes.
5&1 additionally recommends 30 minutes a day of exercise which is likewise important for maintaining weight off and maintaining proper health.

LEAN AND GREEN RECIPES

DELICIOUS ZUCCHINI QUICHE

COOKING: 60' PREPARATION: 15' SERVES: 8

INGREDIENTS

- 6 eggs
- 2 medium zucchini, shredded
- 1/2 tsp. dried basil
- 2 garlic cloves, minced
- 1 tbsp dry onion, minced
- 2 tbsp parmesan cheese, grated
- 2 tbsp fresh parsley, chopped
- 1/2 cup olive oil
- 1 cup cheddar cheese, shredded
- 1/4 cup coconut flour
- 3/4 cup almond flour
- 1/2 tsp. salt

DIRECTIONS

1. Preheat the oven to 350 F.
2. Grease 9-inch pie dish and set aside.
3. Squeeze out excess liquid from zucchini.
4. Add all ingredients into the large bowl and mix until well combined.
5. Pour into the prepared pie dish.
6. Bake in preheated oven for 45-60 minutes or until set.
7. Remove from the oven and let it cool completely.
8. Slice and serve.

NUTRITIONS: Calories: 288 Cal Fat: 26.3 g
Carbohydrates: 5 g Sugar: 1.6 g Protein: 11 g
Cholesterol: 139 mg

CLOUD BREAD

COOKING: 35' PREPARATION: 25' SERVES: 3

INGREDIENTS

» ½ cup of Fat-free 0% Plain Greek Yogurt (4.4 Oz)
» 3 Eggs, Separated
» 16 teaspoon Cream of Tartar
» 1 Packet sweetener (a granulated sweetener just like stevia)

DIRECTIONS

1. For about 30 minutes before making this meal, place the Kitchen Aid Bowl and the whisk attachment in the freezer.
2. Preheat your oven to 30 degrees
3. Remove the mixing bowl and whisk attachment from the freezer
4. Separate the eggs. Now put the egg whites in the Kitchen Aid Bowl, and they should be in a different
5. In the medium-sized bowl containing the yolks, mix in the sweetener and yogurt.
6. In the bowl containing the egg white, add in the cream of tartar. Beat this mixture until the egg whites turn to stiff peaks.
7. Now, take the egg yolk mixture and carefully fold it into the egg whites. Be cautious and avoid over-stirring.
8. Place baking paper on a baking tray and spray with cooking spray.
9. Scoop out 6 equally-sized "blobs" of the "dough" onto the parchment paper.

10. Bake for about 25-35 minutes (make sure you check when it is 25 minutes, in some ovens, they are done at
this timestamp). You will know they are done as they will get brownish at the top and have some crack.
11. Most people like them cold against being warm
12. Most people like to re-heat in a toast oven or toaster to get them a little bit crispy.
13. Your serving size should be about 2 pieces.

NUTRITIONS: Calories: 234 Protein: 23g Carbs: 5g Fiber: 8g Sodium: 223g

AVOCADO LIME SHRIMP SALAD

COOKING: 0' PREPARATION: 15' SERVES: 2

INGREDIENTS

- 14 ounces of jumbo cooked shrimp, peeled and deveined; chopped
- 4 ½ ounces of avocado, diced
- 1 ½ cup of tomato, diced
- ¼ cup of chopped green onion
- ¼ cup of jalapeno with the seeds removed, diced fine
- 1 teaspoon of olive oil
- 2 tablespoons of lime juice
- 1/8 teaspoon of salt
- 1 tablespoon of chopped cilantro

DIRECTIONS

1. Get a small bowl and combine green onion, olive oil, lime juice, pepper, a pinch of salt. Wait for about 5 minutes for all of them to marinate and mellow the flavor of the onion.
2. Get a large bowl and combined chopped shrimp, tomato, avocado, jalapeno. Combine all of the ingredients, add cilantro, and gently toss.
3. Add pepper and salt as desired.

NUTRITIONS: Calories: 314 Protein: 26g Carbs: 15g Fiber: 9g

FUELING RECIPES

HIGH PROTEIN CHIPOTLE CHEDDAR QUESADILLA

COOKING: 10' PREPARATION: 10' SERVES: 4

INGREDIENTS

- Tortillas (4, low carb)
- Cottage cheese (2 cups, low sodium)
- Cheddar cheese (2 cups, low fat, shredded)
- Bell pepper (1, red, thinly sliced)
- Onion (1, thinly sliced)
- Portobello mushrooms (1 cup, thinly sliced)
- Chipotle seasoning (2-3 tbsp)
- Mild salsa (for dipping)

DIRECTIONS

1. Add the bell pepper (sliced, red), onion (sliced) and mushrooms (sliced) into a large grill pan over medi- um heat.
2. Cook for approximately 10 minutes until soft. Re- move then transfer into a bowl (medium). Set aside.
3. Add the chipotle seasoning and cottage cheese in a small bowl. Stir well to incorporate.
4. Place tortillas onto the grill pan and pour vegetable mixture over tortillas.
5. Sprinkle cottage cheese mixture over the top then top off using the cheddar cheese (shredded).
6. Place an additional tortilla over the top of filling.
7. Cook for roughly 2 minutes then flip and continue cooking for a next minute.

8. Repeat process with remaining tortillas and filling.
9. Serve immediately with the salsa (mild).

NUTRITIONS: Calories: 287 Cal Protein: 32.6 g Carbohydrates: 29.8 g Fats: 10.6 g

ZUCCHINI BOATS WITH BEEF AND PIMIENTO ROJO

COOKING: 30' PREPARATION: 10' SERVES: 4

INGREDIENTS

- 4 zucchinis
- 2 tbsp olive oil
- 1 1/2 lb. ground beef
- 1 medium red onion, chopped
- 2 tbsp chopped pimiento
- Pink salt and black pepper to taste
- 1 cup grated yellow cheddar cheese

DIRECTIONS

1. Preheat oven to 350°F.
2. Lay the zucchinis on a flat surface, trim off the ends and cut in half lengthwise. Scoop out the pulp from each half with a spoon to make shells. Chop the pulp.
3. Heat oil in a skillet; add the ground beef, red onion, pimiento, zucchini pulp, and season with salt and black pepper.
4. Cook for 6 minutes while stirring to break up lumps until beef is no longer pink. Turn the heat off.
5. Spoon the beef into the boats and sprinkle with cheddar cheese.
6. Place on a greased baking sheet and cook to melt the cheese for 15 minutes until zucchini boats are tender.
7. Take out, cool for 2 minutes, and serve warm with a mixed green salad.

NUTRITIONS: Calories: 335 Cal Fats: 24 g
Carbohydrates: 7 g Protein: 18 g

CARROT CAKE OATMEAL

COOKING: 15' PREPARATION: 10' SERVES: 1

INGREDIENTS

- 1/8 cup pecans
- 1/2 cup finely shredded carrot
- 1/4 cup old-fashioned oats
- 5/8 cups unsweetened nondairy milk
- 1/2 tablespoon pure maple syrup
- 1/2 teaspoon ground cinnamon
- 1/2 teaspoon ground ginger
- 1/8 teaspoon ground nutmeg
- One tablespoon chia seed

DIRECTIONS

1. Over medium-high heat in a skillet, toast the pecans for 3 to 4 minutes, often stirring, until browned and fragrant (watch closely, as they can burn quickly). Pour the pecans onto a cutting board and coarsely chop them. Set aside.
2. In an 8-quart pot over medium-high heat, combine the carrot, oats, milk, maple syrup, cinnamon, gin- ger, and nutmeg. When it is already boiling, reduce the heat to medium-low. Cook, uncovered, for 10 minutes, stirring occasionally.
3. Stir in the chopped pecans and chia seeds. Serve immediately.

NUTRITIONS: Calories: 307 Fat: 17g Protein: 7g Carbohydrates: 35g Fiber: 11g

SPICED SORGHUM AND BERRIES

COOKING: 1 H PREPARATION: 5' SERVES: 1

INGREDIENTS
- 1/4 cup whole-grain sorghum
- 1/4 teaspoon ground cinnamon
- 1/4 teaspoon Chinese five-spice powder
- 3/4 cups water
- 1/4 cup unsweetened nondairy milk
- 1/4 teaspoon vanilla extract
- 1/2 tablespoons pure maple syrup
- 1/2 tablespoon chia seed
- 1/8 cup sliced almonds
- 1/2 cups fresh raspberries, divided

DIRECTIONS

1. Using a large pot over medium-high heat, stir to- gether the sorghum, cinnamon, five-spice powder, and water. Wait for the water to a boil, cover the bank, and reduce the heat to medium-low. Cook for 1 hour, or until the sorghum is soft and chewy. If the sorghum grains are still hard, add another water cup and cook for 15 minutes more.
2. Using a glass measuring cup, whisk together the milk, vanilla, and maple syrup to blend. Add the mixture to the sorghum and the chia seeds, almonds, and 1 cup of raspberries. Gently stir to combine.
3. When serving, top with the remaining 1 cup of fresh
raspberries.

NUTRITIONS: Calories: 289 Fat: 8g Protein: 9g Carbohydrates: 52g Fiber: 53g

BEST WHOLE WHEAT PANCAKES

COOKING: 20' PREPARATION: 10'SERVES: 1

INGREDIENTS
- » 3/4 tablespoons ground flaxseed
- » Two tablespoons warm water
- » 1/2 cups whole wheat pastry flour
- » 1/8 cup rye flour
- » 1/2 tablespoons double-acting baking powder
- » 1/4 teaspoon ground cinnamon
- » 1/8 teaspoon ground ginger
- » One cup unsweetened nondairy milk
- » 3/4 tablespoons pure maple syrup
- » 1/4 teaspoon vanilla extract

DIRECTIONS

1. Mix the warm water and flaxseed in a large bowl. Set aside for at least 5 minutes.
2. Whisk together the pastry and rye flours, baking powder, cinnamon, and ginger to combine.
3. Whisk together the milk, maple syrup, and vanilla in a large bowl. Make use of a spatula, fold the wet in- gredients into the dry ingredients. Fold in the soaked flaxseed until fully incorporated.
4. Heat a large skillet or nonstick griddle over medi- um-high heat. Working in batches, 3 to 4 pancakes at a time, add 1/4-cup portions of batter to the hot skillet. Until golden brown, cook for 3 to 4 minutes each side or no liquid batter is visible.

NUTRITIONS: Calories: 301 Fat: 4g Protein: 10g Carbohydrates: 57g Fiber: 10g

BREAKFAST

WALNUT CRUNCH BANANA BREAD

COOKING: 1H 30' PREPARATION: 5' SERVES: 1

INGREDIENTS

- 4 ripe bananas
- 1/4 cup maple syrup
- 1 tablespoon apple cider vinegar
- 1 teaspoon vanilla extract
- 1 1/2 cups whole-wheat flour
- 1/2 teaspoon ground cinnamon
- 1/2 teaspoon baking soda
- 1/4 cup walnut pieces (optional)

DIRECTIONS

1. Preheat the oven to 350°F.
2. In a large bowl, use a fork or mixing spoon to mash the bananas until they reach a puréed consistency (small bits of banana are acceptable). Stir in the ma- ple syrup, apple cider vinegar, and vanilla.
3. Stir in the flour, cinnamon, and baking soda. Fold in the walnut pieces (if using).
4. Gently pour the batter into a loaf pan, filling it no more than three-quarters of the way full. Bake for 1 hour, or until you can stick a knife into the middle and it comes out clean.
5. Remove from the oven and allow cooling on the countertop for a minimum of 30 minutes before serving.

NUTRITIONS: Fat: 1g Carbohydrates: 40 g Fiber: 5 g Protein: 4 g

PLANT-POWERED PANCAKES

COOKING: 15' PREPARATION: 5' SERVES: 8

INGREDIENTS

- 1 cup whole-wheat flour
- 1 teaspoon baking powder
- 1/2 teaspoon ground cinnamon
- 1 cup plant-based milk
- 1/2 cup unsweetened applesauce
- 1/4 cup maple syrup
- 1 teaspoon vanilla extract

DIRECTIONS

1. In a large bowl, combine the flour, baking powder, and cinnamon.
2. Stir in the milk, applesauce, maple syrup, and vanilla until no dry flour is left and the batter is smooth.
3. Heat a large, nonstick skillet or griddle over medium heat. For each pancake, pour 1/4 cup of batter onto the hot skillet. Once bubbles form over the top of the pancake and the sides begin to brown, flip and cook for 1 to 2 minutes more.
4. Repeat until all of the batter is used, and serve.

NUTRITIONS: Fat: 2 g Carbohydrates: 44 g Fiber: 5 g Protein: 5 g

LEAN AND GREEN CHICKEN PESTO PASTA

COOKING: 15' PREPARATION: 5' SERVES: 1

INGREDIENTS

- 3 cups of raw kale leaves
- 2 tbsp. of olive oil
- 2 cups of fresh basil
- 1/4 teaspoon salt
- 3 tbsp. lemon juice
- Three garlic cloves
- 2 cups of cooked chicken breast
- 1 cup of baby spinach
- 6 ounce of uncooked chicken pasta
- 3 ounces of diced fresh mozzarella
- Basil leaves or red pepper flakes to garnish

DIRECTIONS

1. Start by making the pesto, add the kale, lemon juice, basil, garlic cloves, olive oil, and salt to a blender and blend until its smooth.
2. Add salt and pepper to taste.
3. Cook the pasta and strain off the water. Reserve 1/4 cup of the liquid.
4. Get a bowl and mix everything, the cooked pasta, pesto, diced chicken, spinach, mozzarella, and the reserved pasta liquid.
5. Sprinkle the mixture with additional chopped basil or red paper flakes (optional).

6.   Now your salad is ready. You may serve it warm or chilled. Also, it can be taken as a salad mix-ins or as a side dish. Leftovers should be stored in the refrigerator inside an air-tight container for 3-5 days.

NUTRITIONS: Calories: 244 Protein: 20.5 g Carbohydrates: 22.5 g Fats: 10 g

CRUNCHY QUINOA MEAL

COOKING: 25 PREPARATION: 5' SERVES: 2

INGREDIENTS

- 3 cups coconut milk
- 1 cup rinsed quinoa
- 1/8 tsp. ground cinnamon
- 1 cup raspberry
- 1/2 cup chopped coconuts

DIRECTIONS

1. In a saucepan, pour milk and bring to a boil over moderate heat.
2. Add the quinoa to the milk and then bring it to a boil once more.
3. You then let it simmer for at least 15 minutes on medium heat until the milk is reduced.
4. Stir in the cinnamon then mix properly.
5. Cover it then cook for 8 minutes until the milk is completely absorbed.
6. Add the raspberry and cook the meal for 30 seconds.
7. Serve and enjoy.

NUTRITIONS: Calories: 271 kcal Fat: 3.7g Carbs: 54g Proteins: 6.5g

COCONUT PANCAKES

COOKING: 15' PREPARATION: 5' SERVES: 4

INGREDIENTS

- 1 cup coconut flour
- 2 tbsps. arrowroot powder
- 1 tsp. baking powder
- 1 cup coconut milk
- 3 tbsps. coconut oil

DIRECTIONS

1. In a medium container, mix in all the dry ingredients.
2. Add the coconut milk and 2 tbsps. of the coconut oil then mix properly.
3. In a skillet, melt 1 tsp. of coconut oil.
4. Pour a ladle of the batter into the skillet then swirl the pan to spread the batter evenly into a smooth pancake.
5. Cook it for like 3 minutes on medium heat until it becomes firm.
6. Turn the pancake to the other side then cook it for another 2 minutes until it turns golden brown.
7. Cook the remaining pancakes in the same process.
8. Serve.

NUTRITIONS: Calories: 377 kcal Fat: 14.9g Carbs: 60.7g Protein: 6.4g

ZUCCHINI PANCAKES

COOKING: 8' PREPARATION: 15' SERVES: 8

INGREDIENTS

- 12 tbsps. alkaline water
- 6 large grated zucchinis
- Sea salt
- 4 tbsps. ground Flax Seeds
- 2 tsps. olive oil
- 2 finely chopped jalapeño peppers
- 1/2 cup finely chopped scallions

DIRECTIONS

1. In a bowl, mix together water and the flax seeds then set it aside.

2. Pour oil in a large non-stick skillet then heat it on medium heat.

3. The add the black pepper, salt, and zucchini.

4. Cook for 3 minutes then transfer the zucchini into a large bowl.

5. Add the flax seed and the scallion's mixture then properly mix it.

6. Preheat a griddle then grease it lightly with the cook- ing spray.

7. Pour 1/4 of the zucchini mixture into griddle then
cook for 3 minutes.

8. Flip the side carefully then cook for 2 more minutes.

9. Repeat the procedure with the remaining mixture in batches.

10. Serve.

NUTRITIONS: Calories: 71 kcal Fat: 2.8g Carbs: 9.8g Protein: 3.7g

SQUASH HASH

COOKING: 10' PREPARATION: 2' SERVES: 2

INGREDIENTS

- 1 tsp. onion powder
- 1/2 cup finely chopped onion
- 2 cups spaghetti squash
- 1/2 tsp. sea salt

DIRECTIONS

1. Using paper towels, squeeze extra moisture from spaghetti squash.
2. Place the squash into a bowl then add the salt, onion, and the onion powder.
3. Stir properly to mix them.
4. Spray a non-stick cooking skillet with cooking spray then place it over moderate heat.
5. Add the spaghetti squash to pan.
6. Cook the squash for about 5 minutes.
7. Flip the hash browns using a spatula.
8. Cook for 5 minutes until the desired crispness is reached.
9. Serve.

NUTRITIONS: Calories: 44 kcal Fat: 0.6g Carbs: 9.7g Protein: 0.9g

MAINS

HERBED WILD RICE

COOKING: 4-6H PREPARATION: 10' SERVES: 8

INGREDIENTS

- 3 cups wild rice, rinsed and drained
- 6 cups Roasted Vegetable Broth
- 1 onion, chopped
- 1/2 teaspoon salt
- 1/2 teaspoon dried thyme leaves
- 1/2 teaspoon dried basil leaves
- 1 bay leaf
- 1/3 cup chopped fresh flat-leaf parsley

DIRECTIONS

1. In a 6-quart slow cooker, mix the wild rice, vegetable broth, onion, salt, thyme, basil, and bay leaf.
2. Cover and cook on low for 4 to 6 hours, or until the wild rice is tender but still firm.
3. You can cook this dish longer until the wild rice pops, taking about 7 to 8 hours.
4. Remove and discard the bay leaf.
5. Stir in the parsley and serve.

NUTRITIONS: Calories: 258 Cal Carbohydrates: 54 g Sugar: 3 g Fiber: 5 g Fat: 2 g Saturated Fat: 0 g Protein: 6 g Sodium: 257 mg

BUFFALO CHICKEN SLIDERS

COOKING: 15' PREPARATION: 10' SERVES: 12

INGREDIENTS

- Chicken breasts (2 lb., cooked, shredded)
- Wing sauce (1 cup)
- Ranch dressing mix (1 pack)
- Blue cheese dressing (1/4 cup, low fat)
- Lettuce (for topping)
- Buns (12, slider)

DIRECTIONS

1. Add the chicken breasts (shredded, cooked) in a large bowl along with the ranch dressing and wing sauce.
2. Stir well to incorporate then place a piece of lettuce onto each slider roll.
3. Top off using chicken mixture.
4. Drizzle blue cheese dressing over chicken then top off using top buns of slider rolls
5. Serve.

NUTRITIONS: Calories: 300 Cal Fat: 14 g Cholesterol: 25 mg

HERBED GARLIC BLACK BEANS

COOKING: 7-9H PREPARATION: 10' SERVES: 8

INGREDIENTS

- 3 cups dried black beans, rinsed and drained
- 2 onions, chopped
- 8 garlic cloves, minced
- 6 cups low-sodium vegetable broth
- 1/2 teaspoon salt
- 1 teaspoon dried basil leaves
- 1/2 teaspoon dried thyme leaves
- 1/2 teaspoon dried oregano leaves

DIRECTIONS

1. In a 6-quart slow cooker, mix all the ingredients.
2. Cover and cook on low for 7 to 9 hours, or until the beans have absorbed the liquid and are tender.
3. Remove and discard the bay leaf

NUTRITIONS: Calories: 250 Cal Carbohydrates: 47 g Sugar: 3 g Fiber: 17 g Fat: 0 g Satu- rated Fat: 0 g Protein: 15 g Sodium: 253 mg

QUINOA WITH VEGETABLES

COOKING: 5-6H PREPARATION: 10' SERVES: 8

INGREDIENTS

- 2 cups quinoa, rinsed and drained
- 2 onions, chopped
- 2 carrots, peeled and sliced
- 1 cup sliced cremini mushrooms
- 3 garlic cloves, minced
- 4 cups low-sodium vegetable broth
- 1/2 teaspoon salt
- 1 teaspoon dried marjoram leaves
- 1/8 teaspoon freshly ground black pepper

DIRECTIONS

1. In a 6-quart slow cooker, mix all of the ingredients.
2. Cover and cook on low for 5 to 6 hours, or until the quinoa and vegetables are tender.
3. Stir the mixture and serve.

NUTRITIONS: Calories: 204 Cal Carbohydrates: 35 g Sugar: 4 g Fiber: 4 g Fat: 3 g Saturated Fat: 0 g Protein: 7 g Sodium: 229 mg

GREEK STYLE QUESADILLAS

COOKING: 10' PREPARATION: 10' SERVES: 4

INGREDIENTS

- 4 whole wheat tortillas
- 1 cup Mozzarella cheese, shredded
- 1 cup fresh spinach, chopped
- 2 tablespoon Greek yogurt
- 1 egg, beaten
- ¼ cup green olives, sliced
- 1 tablespoon olive oil
- 1/3 cup fresh cilantro, chopped

DIRECTIONS

1. In the bowl, combine together Mozzarella cheese, spinach, yogurt, egg, olives, and cilantro.
2. Then pour olive oil in the skillet.
3. In the skillet Place one tortilla and spread it with Mozzarella mixture.
4. Top it with the second tortilla and spread it with cheese mixture again.
5. Then place the third tortilla and spread it with all remaining cheese mixture.
6. Cover it with the last tortilla and fry it for 5 minutes from each side over the medium heat.

NUTRITIONS: Calories: 193 Fat: 7.7g Fiber: 3.2g Carbs: 23.6g Protein: 8.3g

LIGHT PAPRIKA MOUSSAKA

COOKING: 45' PREPARATION: 15' SERVES: 3

INGREDIENTS

- 1 eggplant, trimmed
- 1 cup ground chicken
- 1/3 cup white onion, diced
- 3 oz. Cheddar cheese, shredded
- 1 potato, sliced
- 1 teaspoon olive oil
- 1 teaspoon salt
- ½ cup milk
- 1 tablespoon butter
- 1 tablespoon ground paprika
- 1 tablespoon Italian seasoning
- 1 teaspoon tomato paste

DIRECTIONS

1. Slice the eggplant in length and sprinkle with salt.
2. In the skillet Pour olive oil and add sliced potato.
3. Roast potato for 2 minutes from each side.
4. Then transfer it in the plate.
5. Put eggplant in the skillet and roast it for 2 minutes from each side too.
6. In the pan Pour milk and bring it to boil.
7. Add tomato paste, Italian seasoning, paprika, butter, and Cheddar cheese.
8. Then mix up together onion with ground chicken.

9. Arrange the sliced potato in the casserole in one layer.
10. Then add ½ part of all sliced eggplants.
11. Spread the eggplants with ½ part of chicken mixture.
12. Then add remaining eggplants.
13. Pour the milk mixture over the eggplants.
14. Bake moussaka for 30 minutes at 355F.

NUTRITIONS: Calories: 387 Fat: 21g Fiber: 8.9g Carbs: 26.6g Protein: 25.3g

PROSCIUTTO WRAPPED MOZZARELLA BALLS

COOKING: 10' PREPARATION: 10' SERVES: 4

INGREDIENTS

- 8 Mozzarella balls, cherry size
- 4 oz. bacon, sliced
- ¼ teaspoon ground black pepper
- ¾ teaspoon dried rosemary
- 1 teaspoon butter

DIRECTIONS

1. Sprinkle the sliced bacon with ground black pepper
and dried rosemary.
2. Wrap every Mozzarella ball in the sliced bacon and
secure them with toothpicks.
3. Melt butter.
4. Brush wrapped Mozzarella balls with butter.
5. Line the baking tray with the parchment and arrange
Mozzarella balls in it.
6. Bake the meal for 10 minutes at 365F.

NUTRITIONS: Calories: 323 Fat: 26.8 Fiber: 0.1 Carbs: 0.6 Protein: 20.6

SNACKS RECIPES

EGGPLANT DIP

COOKING: 40' PREPARATION: 10' SERVES: 4

INGREDIENTS

- 1 eggplant, poked with a fork
- 2 tablespoons tahini paste
- 2 tablespoons lemon juice
- 2 garlic cloves, minced
- 1 tablespoon olive oil
- Salt and black pepper to the taste
- 1 tablespoon parsley, chopped

DIRECTIONS

1. Put the eggplant in a roasting pan, bake at 400° F for 40 minutes, cool down, peel and transfer to your food processor.
2. Add the rest of the remaining ingredients except the parsley, pulse well, divide into small bowls and serve as an appetizer with the parsley sprinkled on top.

NUTRITIONS: Calories 121 Fat 4.3 g Fiber 1 g Carbs 1.4 g Protein 4.3 g

BULGUR LAMB MEATBALLS

COOKING: 15' PREPARATION: 10' SERVES: 6

INGREDIENTS

- 1 and ½ cups Greek yogurt
- ½ teaspoon cumin, ground
- 1 cup cucumber, shredded
- ½ teaspoon garlic, minced
- A pinch of salt and black pepper
- 1 cup bulgur
- 2 cups water
- 1 pound lamb, ground
- ¼ cup parsley, chopped
- ¼ cup shallots, chopped
- ½ teaspoon allspice, ground
- ½ teaspoon cinnamon powder
- 1 tablespoon olive oil

DIRECTIONS

1. Combine the bulgur with the water in a bowl, cover the bowl, leave aside for 10 minutes, drain and trans- fer to a bowl.
2. Add the meat, the yogurt and the rest of the ingredients except the oil, stir well and shape medium meatballs out of this mix.
3. Heat oil in a pan over medium-high heat, add the meatballs, cook them for 7 minutes on each side, arrange them all on a platter and serve as an appetizer.

NUTRITIONS: Calories 300 Fat 9.6 g Fiber 4.6 g Carbs 22.6 g Protein 6.6 g

CUCUMBER ROLLS

COOKING: 0' PREPARATION: 5' SERVES: 6

INGREDIENTS

- » 1 big cucumber, sliced lengthwise
- » 1 tablespoon parsley, chopped
- » 8 ounces canned tuna, drained and mashed
- » Salt and black pepper to the taste
- » 1 teaspoon lime juice

DIRECTIONS

1. Arrange cucumber slices on a working surface, di- vide the rest of the ingredients, and roll.
2. Arrange all the rolls on a surface and serve as an appetizer.

NUTRITIONS: Calories 200 Fat 6 g Fiber 3.6 g Carbs 7.6 g Protein 3.6 g

FETA ARTICHOKE DIP

COOKING: 30' PREPARATION: 10' SERVES: 8

INGREDIENTS

- 8 ounces artichoke hearts, drained and quartered
- ¾ cup basil, chopped
- ¾ cup green olives, pitted and chopped
- 1 cup parmesan cheese, grated
- 5 ounces feta cheese, crumbled

DIRECTIONS

1. In your food processor, mix the artichokes with the basil and the rest of the ingredients, pulse well, and transfer to a baking dish.
2. Introduce in the oven, bake at 375° F for 30 minutes
and serve as a party dip.

NUTRITIONS: Calories 186 Fat 12.4 g Fiber 0.9 g Carbs 2.6 g Protein 1.5 g

CHEESEBURGER PIE

COOKING: 90' PREPARATION: 20' SERVES: 4

INGREDIENTS

- 1 large spaghetti squash
- 1 lb. lean ground beef
- 1/4 cup diced onion
- 2 eggs
- 1/3 cup low-fat, plain Greek yogurt
- 2 Tbsp. Tomato sauce
- 1/2 tsp. Worcestershire sauce
- 2/3 cup reduced-fat, shredded cheddar cheese
- 2 oz. dill pickle slices
- Cooking spray

DIRECTIONS

1. Preheat oven to 400°F. Slice spaghetti squash in half lengthwise; dismiss pulp and seeds.
2. Spray insides with cooking spray.
3. Place squash halves cut-side- down onto a foil-lined baking sheet, and bake for 30 minutes.
4. Once cooked, let cool to before scraping squash flesh with a fork to remove spaghetti-like strands; set aside.
5. Push squash strands in the bottom and up sides of the greased pie pan, cre- ating an even layer.
6. Meanwhile, set up pie filling.
7. In a lightly greased, medium-sized skillet, cook beef and onion over medium heat 8 to 10 minutes, sometimes stirring, until meat is brown.
8. Drain and remove from heat.

9. In a medium-sized bowl, whisk together eggs, tomato paste, Greek yogurt, and Worcestershire sauce. Stir in ground beef mixture.
10. Pour pie filling over squash crust.
11. Sprinkle meat filling with cheese, and then top with dill pickle slices.
12. Bake for 40 minutes.

NUTRITIONS: Calories: 409 Cal Fat: 24.49 g Carbohydrates: 15.06 g Protein: 30.69 g

CHICKEN AND MUSHROOMS

COOKING: 15' PREPARATION: 10' SERVES: 6

INGREDIENTS

- 2 Breast of Chicken
- 1 Cup of sliced white champignons
- 1 Cup of sliced green chilies
- 1/2 cup scallions hacked
- 1 Teaspoon of chopped garlic
- 1 cup of low-fat cheddar shredded cheese (1-1,5 lb. grams fat / ounce)
- 1 Tablespoon of olive oil
- 1 Tablespoon of butter

DIRECTIONS

1. Fry the chicken breasts with olive oil.
2. When needed, salt and pepper.
3. Grill breasts of chicken in a plate with grill.
4. For every serving weigh 4 ounces of chicken. (Makes 2 servings, leftovers save for another meal).
5. In a butter pan, stir in mushrooms, green peppers, scallions and garlic until smooth, and a little dark.
6. Place the chicken in a baking platter.
7. Cover with mushroom combination.
8. Top on ham.
9. Place the cheese in a 350 * oven until it melts.

NUTRITIONS: Carbohydrates: 2 g Protein: 23 g Fat: 11 g Cholesterol: 112 mg Sodium: 198 mg Potassium: 261 mg

BAKED BEEF ZUCCHINI

COOKING: 40' PREPARATION: 10' SERVES: 4

INGREDIENTS

- 2 large zucchini
- 1 cup minced beef
- 1 cup mushroom, chopped
- 1 tomato, chopped
- 1/2 cup spinach, chopped
- 1 tbsp chives, minced
- 2 tbsp olive oil
- Salt and pepper to taste
- 1 tbsp almond butter
- 1 tsp. garlic powder
- 1 cup cheddar cheese, grated
- 1/3 tsp. ginger powder

DIRECTIONS

1. Preheat the oven to 400 degrees F.
2. Add aluminum foil on a baking sheet.
3. Cut the zucchini in half. Scoop out the seeds and make pockets to stuff it later.
4. In a pan, add the olive oil.
5. Toss the beef until brown.
6. Add the mushroom, tomato, chives, salt, pepper, garlic, ginger, and spinach.
7. Cook for 2 minutes. Take off the heat.
8. Stuff the zucchinis using the mix.
9. Add them onto the baking sheet. Sprinkle the cheese
on top.

10. Add the butter on top. Bake for 30 minutes. Serve warm.

NUTRITIONS: Fat: 12.8 g Cholesterol: 79.7 mg Sodium: 615.4 mg Potassium: 925.8 mg Carbohydrate: 26.8 g

COBB SALAD WITH BLUE CHEESE DRESSING

COOKING: 30' PREPARATION: 15' SERVES: 6

INGREDIENTS

- Dressing:
- 1/2 cup buttermilk
- 1 cup mayonnaise
- 2 tbsp Worcestershire sauce
- 1/2 cup sour cream
- 1 1/2 cup crumbled blue cheese
- Salt and black pepper to taste
- 2 tbsp chopped chives
- Salad:
- 6 eggs
- 2 chicken breasts, boneless and skinless
- 5 strips bacon
- 1 iceberg lettuce, cut into chunks
- 1 romaine lettuce, chopped
- 1 bibb lettuce, cored and leaves removed
- 2 avocado, pitted and diced
- 2 large tomatoes, chopped
- 1/2 cup crumbled blue cheese
- 2 scallions, chopped

DIRECTIONS

1. In a bowl, whisk the buttermilk, mayonnaise, Worcestershire sauce, and sour cream.
2. Stir in the blue cheese, salt, black pepper, and chives.
Place in the refrigerator to chill until ready to use.

3. Bring the eggs to boil in salted water over medium
heat for 10 minutes.
4. Once ready, drain the eggs and transfer to the ice
bath. Peel and chop the eggs. Set aside.
5. Preheat the grill pan over high heat. Season the chicken with salt and pepper.
6. Grill for 3 minutes on each side. Remove to a plate to
cool for 3 minutes, and cut into bite-size chunks.
7. Fry the bacon in another pan set over medium heat until crispy, about 6 minutes. Remove, let cool for 2 minutes, and chop.
8. Arrange the lettuce leaves in a salad bowl and add the avocado, tomatoes, eggs, bacon, and chicken in single piles.
9. Sprinkle the blue cheese over the salad as well as the
scallions and black pepper.
10. Drizzle the blue cheese dressing on the salad and
serve with low carb bread.

NUTRITIONS: Calories: 122 Cal Fats: 14 g Carbohydrates: 2 g Protein: 23

VEGETABLES

SWEET POTATO CHIPS

COOKING: 10' PREPARATION: 5' SERVES: 4

INGREDIENTS

- 2 large sweet potatoes, cut into strips 25 mm thick
- 15 ml of oil
- 10g of salt
- 2g black pepper
- 2g of paprika
- 2g garlic powder
- 2g onion powder

DIRECTIONS

1. Cut the sweet potatoes into strips 25 mm thick.
2. Preheat the air fryer for a few minutes.
3. Add the cut sweet potatoes in a large bowl and mix with the oil until the potatoes are all evenly coated.
4. Sprinkle salt, black pepper, paprika, garlic powder and onion powder. Mix well.
5. Place the French fries in the preheated baskets and cook for 10 minutes at 205°C. Be sure to shake the baskets halfway through cooking.

NUTRITIONS: Calories: 123 Carbs: 2 g Fat: 11 g Protein: 4 g Fiber: 0 g

FRIED ZUCCHINI

COOKING: 8' PREPARATION: 10' SERVES: 4

INGREDIENTS

- 2 medium zucchinis, cut into strips 19 mm thick
- 60g all-purpose flour
- 12g of salt
- 2g black pepper
- 2 beaten eggs
- 15 ml of milk
- 84g Italian seasoned breadcrumbs
- 25g grated Parmesan cheese
- Nonstick Spray Oil
- Ranch sauce, to serve

DIRECTIONS

1. Cut the zucchini into strips 19 mm thick.
2. Mix with the flour, salt, and pepper on a plate. Mix the eggs and milk in a separate dish. Put breadcrumbs and Parmesan cheese in another dish.
3. Cover each piece of zucchini with flour, then dip them in egg and pass them through the crumbs. Leave aside.
4. Preheat the air fryer, set it to 175°C.
5. Place the covered zucchini in the preheated air fryer and spray with oil spray. Set the timer to 8 minutes and press Start / Pause.
6. Be sure to shake the baskets in the middle of cooking.
7. Serve with tomato sauce or ranch sauce.

NUTRITIONS: Calories: 68 Carbs: 2 g Fat: 11 g Protein: 4 g Fiber: 143g

CAULIFLOWER CRUST PIZZA

COOKING: 45' PREPARATION: 20' SERVES: 4

INGREDIENTS

» I cauliflower (it should be cut into smaller portions).
» 1/4 grated parmesan cheese
» 1 egg
» 1Tsp Italian seasoning
» 1/4 Tsp. kosher salt
» 2 cups of freshly grated mozzarella
» 1/4 cup of spicy pizza sauce.
» Basil leaves, for garnishing.

DIRECTIONS

1. Begin by preheating your oven while using the parchment paper to rim the baking sheet.
2. Process the cauliflower into a fine powder, and then transfer to a bowl, before putting it into the micro- wave.
3. Leave for about 5-6 minutes to get it soft.
4. Transfer the microwave cauliflower to a clean and
dry kitchen towel.
5. Leave it to cool off.
6. When cold, use the kitchen towel to wrap the cauliflower and then get rid of all the moisture by wringing the
towel.
7. Continue squeezing until water is gone completely. Put the cauliflower, Italian seasoning, Parmesan, egg, salt, and mozzarella (1 cup).

8. Stir very well until well combined.
9. Transfer the combined mixture to the baking sheet previously prepared, pressing it into a 10-inch round shape. Bake for 10-15 minutes until it becomes golden in color. Take the baked crust out of the oven and use the spicy pizza sauce and mozzarella (the leftover 1 cup) to top it.
10. Bake again for 10 more minutes until the cheese melts and looks bubbly. Garnish using fresh basil leaves, you can also enjoy this with salad.

NUTRITIONS: Calories: 74 Cal Carbohydrates: 4 g Protein: 6 g Fat: 4 g Fiber: 2 g

THAI ROASTED VEGGIES

COOKING: 6-8H PREPARATION: 20' SERVES: 8

INGREDIENTS

- » 4 large carrots, peeled and cut into chunks
- » 2 onions, peeled and sliced
- » 6 garlic cloves, peeled and sliced
- » 2 parsnips, peeled and sliced
- » 2 jalapeño peppers, minced
- » 1/2 cup Roasted Vegetable Broth
- » 1/3 cup canned coconut milk
- » 3 tablespoons lime juice
- » 2 tablespoons grated fresh ginger root
- » 2 teaspoons curry powder

DIRECTIONS

1. In a 6-quart slow cooker, mix the carrots, onions, garlic, parsnips, and jalapeño peppers.
2. In a small bowl, mix the vegetable broth, coconut milk, lime juice, ginger root, and curry powder until well blended. Pour this mixture into the slow cooker.
3. Cover and cook on low for 6 to 8 hours, do it until
the vegetables are tender when pierced with a fork.

NUTRITIONS: Calories: 69 Cal Carbohydrates: 13 g Sugar: 6 g Fiber: 3 g Fat: 3g Saturated Fat: 3g Protein: 1g Sodium: 95mg

CRISPY-TOPPED BAKED VEGETABLES

COOKING: 40' PREPARATION: 10' SERVES: 4

INGREDIENTS

- 2 tbsp olive oil
- 1 onion, chopped
- 1 celery stalk, chopped
- 2 carrots, grated
- 1/2-pound turnips, sliced
- 1 cup vegetable broth
- 1 tsp. turmeric
- Sea salt and black pepper, to taste
- 1/2 tsp. liquid smoke
- 1 cup Parmesan cheese, shredded
- 2 tbsp fresh chives, chopped

DIRECTIONS

1. Set oven to 360ºF and grease a baking dish with olive oil.
2. Set a skillet over medium heat and warm olive oil.
3. Sweat the onion until soft, and place in the turnips, carrots and celery; and cook for 4 minutes.
4. Remove the vegetable mixture to the baking dish.
5. Combine vegetable broth with turmeric, pepper, liquid smoke, and salt.
6. Spread this mixture over the vegetables.
7. Sprinkle with Parmesan cheese and bake for about
30 minutes.
8. Garnish with chives to serve.

NUTRITIONS: Calories: 242 Cal Fats: 16.3 g
Carbohydrates: 8.6 g Protein: 16.3 g

MEAT

TOMATO BRAISED CAULIFLOWER WITH CHICKEN

COOKING: 30' PREPARATION: 5' SERVES: 4

INGREDIENTS

- 4 garlic cloves, sliced
- 3 scallions, to be trimmed and cut into 1-inch pieces
- 1/4 teaspoon of dried oregano
- 1/4 teaspoon of crushed red pepper flakes
- 4 1/2 cups of cauliflower
- 1 1/2 cups of diced canned tomatoes
- 1 cup of fresh basil, gently torn
- 1/2 teaspoon each of pepper and salt, divided
- 1 1/2 teaspoon of olive oil
- 1 1/2 lb. of boneless, skinless chicken breasts

DIRECTIONS

1. Get a saucepan and combine the garlic, scallions, oregano, crushed red pepper, cauliflower, tomato, and add 1/4 cup of water.
2. Get everything boil together, add 1/4 teaspoon of pepper and salt for seasoning, and then cover the pot with a lid.
3. Let it simmer for 10 minutes and stir as often as pos- sible until you observe that the cauliflower is tender.
4. Now, wrap up the seasoning with the remaining 1/4 teaspoon of pepper and salt.

5. Toss the chicken breast with olive oil and let it roast in the oven with the heat of 4500F for 20 minutes and an internal temperature of 1650F.
6. Allow the chicken to rest for like 10 minutes.
7. Now slice the chicken, and serve on a bed of tomato

NUTRITIONS: Calories 290 Cal Fat: 10 g
Carbobhryadisreadtecasu:l1ifl3ogwePrr. otein: 38 g

CUMIN-LIME STEAK

COOKING: 30' PREPARATION: 30' SERVES: 4

INGREDIENTS

- Seaweed
- 20 Once. Steak with lean rib-eye
- 6 Tops of Broccoli
- 1 Pack of quick bovine soup (prepared as directed) or 1/2 cup of beef broth
- 1/4 tablespoon lime juice
- 1 1/2 spoonful of ground cumin
- 1 1/2 spoonful of ground coriander
- 2 Big, finely chopped cloves of garlic
- 3 Pounds of olive oil

DIRECTIONS

1. Mix all marinade ingredients (except oil) together in a blender.
2. Add oil to mixer with motor working slowly.
3. Refrigerate and cover until ready to use. Pour 1 cup of marinade over steaks in a glass dish, covering with all sides.
4. Cover and leave to cool for 6 hours (or overnight).
5. Grill over medium-sized coals, turning regularly and clean with 1/2 cup marinade left over.
6. Steam broccoli on the side and serve.

NUTRITIONS: Fats: 0.7 g Sodium: 6.1 mg Carbohydrates: 4.5 g

MEDITERRANEAN GRILLED CHICKEN

COOKING: 2H 20' PREPARATION: 20' SERVES: 4

INGREDIENTS

- 2 tbsp. of olive oil
- 3 spoons full of white cider vinegar
- 1 Italian Seasoning Teaspoon
- 1 A garlic clove
- 1/4 cubic teaspoon black pepper
- One half lemon zest
- 1 Tablespoon of sun-dried, diced tomatoes
- Excellent for salt and pepper
- 14 Once. Non skinless chicken breast
- Summer squash: 3/4 cup
- 3/4 Cup Cockroach
- Oregano (with option)

DIRECTIONS

1. Combine all ingredients (except chicken) into a large plastic bag with a zip-top.
2. Add marinade to chicken, seal bag and coat meat.
3. For extra flavor, cool down for 30 minutes or longer.
4. Remove from marinade chicken, and discard mari- nade.
5. Grill the chicken for 6-7 minutes per side over medi- um heat or until cooked.
6. Place the zucchini and squash on grill (if necessary, on top of the foil).
7. Sprinkle with the flour, oregano and pepper.
8. Switch to cooking thoroughly once.

NUTRITIONS: Carbohydrates: 7 g Protein: 33 g Fat: 23 g Cholesterol: 97 mg Sodium: 301 mg Potassium: 762 mg

SOUPS

QUICK LENTIL CHILI

COOKING: 1H 10' PREPARATION: 15' SERVES: 10

INGREDIENTS

- 1 1/2 cups of seeded or diced pepper
- 1 1/2 cups of coarsely chopped onions 5 cups of vegetable broth (it should have a low sodium content)
- 1 tablespoon of garlic
- 1/4 teaspoon of freshly ground pepper
- 1 cup of red lentils
- 3 filled teaspoons of chili powder
- 1 tablespoon of grounded cumin

DIRECTIONS

1. Place your pot over medium heat
2. Combine your onions, red peppers, low sodium vegetable broth, garlic, salt and pepper
3. Cook and stir always until the onions are more trans-lucent and all the liquid evaporated. This will take about 10mins.
4. Add the remaining broth, lime juice, chili powder, lentils, cumin and boil.
5. Reduce heat at this point, cover it for about 15minutes to shimmer until the lentils are appropriately cooked
6. Add a little water if the mixture seems to be thick.
7. The chili will be appropriately done when most of the water is absorbed.
8. Serve and enjoy.

NUTRITIONS: Protein: 2.3 g Carbohydrates: 12.1 g Dietary Fiber: 3.3 g Sugars: 6.1 g Fat:2.9 g

LEMON GARLIC OREGANO CHICKEN WITH ASPARAGUS

COOKING: 45' PREPARATION: 5' SERVES: 4

INGREDIENTS

» 1 small lemon, juiced (this should be about 2 tablespoons of lemon juice)
» 1 3/4 lb. of bone-in, skinless chicken thighs
» 2 tablespoons of fresh oregano, minced
» 2 cloves of garlic, minced
» 2 lbs. of asparagus, trimmed
» 1/4 teaspoon each or less for black pepper and salt

DIRECTIONS

1. Preheat the oven to about 3500F. Put the chicken in
a medium-sized bowl.
2. Now, add the garlic, oregano, lemon juice, pepper, and salt and toss together to combine.
3. Roast the chicken in the oven until it reaches an internal temperature of 1650F in about 40 minutes.
4. Once the chicken thighs have been cooked, remove and keep aside to rest.
5. Now, steam the asparagus on a stovetop or in a microwave to the desired doneness.
6. Serve asparagus with the roasted chicken thighs.

NUTRITIONS: Calories: 350 Cal Fat: 10 g Carbohydrates: 10 g Protein: 32 g

EASY CAULIFLOWER SOUP

COOKING: 15' PREPARATION: 5' SERVES: 4

INGREDIENTS

- 2 tbsp olive oil
- 2 onions, finely chopped
- 1 tsp. garlic, minced
- 1 pound cauliflower, cut into florets
- 1 cup kale, chopped
- 4 cups vegetable broth
- 1/2 cup almond milk
- 1/2 tsp. salt
- 1/2 tsp. red pepper flakes
- 1 tbsp fresh chopped parsley

DIRECTIONS

1. Set a pot over medium heat and warm the oil.
2. Add garlic and onions and sauté until browned and softened.
3. Place in vegetable broth, kale, and cauliflower; cook for 10 minutes until the mixture boils.
4. Stir in the pepper flakes, salt, and almond milk; re- duce the heat and simmer the soup for 5 minutes.
5. Transfer the soup to an immersion blender and blend to achieve the desired consistency; top with parsley and serve immediately.

NUTRITIONS: Calories: 172 Cal Fats: 10.3 g
Carbohydrates: 11.8g Protein: 8.1 g

SMOOTHIES

CANTALOUPE KALE SMOOTHIE

COOKING: 5' PREPARATION: 5' SERVES: 2

INGREDIENTS

- 8 oz. water
- 1 orange, peeled
- 3 cups kale, chopped
- 1 banana, peeled
- 2 cups cantaloupe, chopped
- 1 zucchini, chopped

DIRECTIONS

1. Toss all your ingredients into your blender then process till smooth and creamy.
2. Serve immediately and enjoy.

NUTRITIONS: Calories: 203 Fat: 0.5g Carbs: 49.2g Protein: 5.6g Fiber: 0g

MIX BERRY CANTALOUPE SMOOTHIE

COOKING: 5' PREPARATION: 5' SERVES: 2

INGREDIENTS

- 1 cup alkaline water
- 2 fresh Seville orange juices
- ¼ cup fresh mint leaves
- 1 ½ cups mixed berries
- 2 cups cantaloupe

DIRECTIONS

1. Toss all your ingredients into your blender then process till smooth.
2. Serve immediately and enjoy.

NUTRITIONS: Calories: 122 Fat: 1g Carbs: 26.1g Protein: 2.4g Fiber: 0g

SOURSOP SMOOTHIE

COOKING: 5' PREPARATION: 5' SERVES: 2

INGREDIENTS

- 3 quartered frozen Burro Bananas
- 1-1/2 cups of Homemade Coconut Milk
- 1/4 cup of Walnuts
- 1 teaspoon of Sea Moss Gel
- 1 teaspoon of Ground Ginger
- 1 teaspoon of Soursop Leaf Powder
- 1 handful of Kale

DIRECTIONS

1. Prepare and put all ingredients in a blender or a food processor.
2. Blend it well until you reach a smooth consistency.
3. Serve and enjoy your Soursop Smoothie!
4. Useful Tips:
5. If you don't have frozen Bananas, you can use fresh ones.

NUTRITIONS: Calories: 213 Fat: 3.1g Carbs: 6g Protein: 8g Fiber: 4.3g

CUCUMBER-GINGER WATER

COOKING: 5' PREPARATION: 5' SERVES: 2

INGREDIENTS

» 1 sliced Cucumber
» 1 smashed thumb of Ginger Root
» 2 cups of Spring Water

DIRECTIONS

1. Prepare and put all ingredients in a jar with a lid.
2. Let the water infuse overnight. Store it in the refrigerator.
3. Serve and enjoy your Cucumber-Ginger Water throughout the day!

NUTRITIONS: Calories: 117 Fat: 2g Carbs: 6g Protein: 8g Fiber: 2

DESSERTS

5&1 GRANOLA

COOKING: 8' PREPARATION: 5' SERVES: 3

INGREDIENTS

- 1 package Oatmeal
- 1 packet stevia
- 1 teaspoon vanilla extract
- 1/2 teaspoon apple spice or pumpkin pie spice

DIRECTIONS

1. Preheat the oven to 4000F. In a bowl, combine all ingredients and add enough water to get the granola to stick together.
2. Drop the granola onto a cookie sheet lined with parchment paper.
3. Bake for 8 minutes but make sure to give the granola a fair shake for even browning halfway through the cooking time.

NUTRITIONS: Calories per serving: 209 Cal Protein: 5.8 g Carbohydrates: 42 g Fat: 3.2 g Sugar: 6.2 g

BROWNIE BITES

COOKING: 0' PREPARATION: 20' SERVES: 13

INGREDIENTS

- 1/4 cup unsweetened chocolate chips
- 1/4 cup unsweetened cocoa powder
- 1 cup pecans, chopped
- 1/2 cup almond butter
- 1/2 tsp vanilla
- 1/4 cup monk fruit sweetener
- 1/8 tsp pink salt

DIRECTIONS

1. Add pecans, sweetener, vanilla, almond butter, cocoa powder, and salt into the food processor and process until well combined.
2. Transfer brownie mixture into the large bowl. Add chocolate chips and fold well.
3. Make small round shape balls from brownie mixture and place onto a baking tray.
4. Place in the freezer for 20 minutes.
5. Serve and enjoy.

NUTRITIONS: Calories: 108 Fat: 9 g Carbs: 4 g Sugar: 1 g Protein: 2 g Cholesterol: 0 mg

PUMPKIN BALLS

COOKING: 0' PREPARATION: 15' SERVES: 18

INGREDIENTS

- 1 cup almond butter
- 5 drops liquid stevia
- 2 tbsp coconut flour
- 2 tbsp pumpkin puree
- 1 tsp pumpkin pie spice

DIRECTIONS

1. Mix together pumpkin puree in a large bowl, and almond butter until well combined.
2. Add liquid stevia, pumpkin pie spice, and coconut flour and mix well.
3. Make small balls from mixture and place onto a baking tray.
4. Place in the freezer for 1 hour.
5. Serve and enjoy.

NUTRITIONS: Calories: 96 Fat: 8 g Carbs: 4 g Sugar: 1 g Protein: 2 g Cholesterol: 0 Mg

CHOCOLATE FROSTY

COOKING: 0' PREPARATION: 20' SERVES: 4

INGREDIENTS

- 2 tbsp unsweetened cocoa powder
- 1 cup heavy whipping cream
- 1 tbsp almond butter
- 5 drops liquid stevia
- 1 tsp vanilla

DIRECTIONS

1. Add cream into the medium bowl and beat using the hand mixer for 5 minutes.
2. Add remaining ingredients and blend until thick cream form.
3. Pour in serving bowls and place them in the freezer for 30 minutes.
4. Serve and enjoy.

NUTRITIONS: Calories: 137 Fat: 13 g Carbs: 3 g Sugar: 0.5 g Protein: 2 g Cholesterol:

PEANUT BUTTER FUDGE

COOKING: 10' PREPARATION: 10' SERVES: 20

INGREDIENTS
- 1/4 cup almonds, toasted and chopped
- 12 oz smooth peanut butter
- 15 drops liquid stevia
- 3 tbsp coconut oil
- 4 tbsp coconut cream
- Pinch of salt

DIRECTIONS

1. Line baking tray with parchment paper.
2. Melt coconut oil in a pan over low heat. Add peanut butter, coconut cream, stevia, and salt in a saucepan. Stir well.
3. Pour fudge mixture into the prepared baking tray and sprinkle chopped almonds on top.
4. Place the tray in the refrigerator for 1 hour or until set.
5. Slice and serve.

NUTRITIONS: Calories: 131 Fat: 12 g Carbs: 4 g Sugar: 2 g Protein: 5 g Cholesterol: 0 mg

EASTER BUNNY

COOKING: 30' PREPARATION: 25' SERVES: 2

INGREDIENTS

- 170 g butter
- 1 1/4 cups icing sugar mixture
- 1 tsp. vanilla extract
- 1 pinch salt
- 3 egg yolks
- 2 1/2 cups plain flour
- 12 marshmallows
- 24 Nestle Smarties pink
- 72 Ferrero Tic Tacs pink
- 3 drops liquid food coloring pink
- Royal Icing
- 2 egg whites
- 2 tsp. lemon juice
- 3 cups icing sugar sifted

DIRECTIONS

1. Preheat the oven to a hundred and 158F.

2. Whisk the butter using hand until it is smooth and creamy.

3. Blend within the icing sugar then add the egg yolks,
vanilla, and salt. Stir until blended.

4. Add the flour and blend it loosely with a wooden spoon till the dough comes together.

5. Turn it out onto a floured surface and knead until
the dough is smooth.

6. Shape it into a disc and wrap it in cling wrap.

7. Refrigerate the dough for 30 minutes.

8. Roll out the dough to about 1 cm thick. Use a 5-6cm round cookie cutter to cut 12 bunny butt shapes out
of the dough. Then use a small egg-shaped cookie cutter to create 24 bunny feet.

9. Place the cookies onto two baking trays lined with baking paper.

10. Bake in the oven for 10-15 minutes until the edges turned browned.

11. Cool on a cooling rack while you make some royal icing.

12. Divide the icing into two halves. Color one half with a few drops of rose food coloring to make it very light
bunny pink.

13. Ice half of your biscuits with pink and half white. Add two bunny's feet to each circle. Add a marshmallow
tail and then a Smartie as a paw pad and three tic tacs for the paw toes.

14. Icing:

15. The use of an electric powered mixer, whisk egg whites with the lemon juice till blended.

16. Regularly upload in sifted icing sugar on low pace till clean.

17. Add meals color of your preference.

18. Pipe onto bunny biscuits.

19. Leave for 2-3 hours to set difficult.

NUTRITIONS: Fat: 41 g Protein: 12 g Cholesterol: 20 mg Carbohydrates: 20 g Sodium: 504 Mg

www.ingramcontent.com/pod-product-compliance
Lightning Source LLC
Chambersburg PA
CBHW071523080526
44588CB00011B/1540